NORTH CAROLINA
STATE BOARD OF COMMUNITY
ENGLISH SPORTS AND RECREATIONS
SOUTHEASTERN COMMUNITY COLLEGE

P9-DHA-886

English Sports and Recreations

BY LILLY C. STONE

FOLGER BOOKS

Published by
THE FOLGER SHAKESPEARE LIBRARY

ALTHOUGH sports and pastimes in Shakespeare's age were far less highly organized than they are today, human nature was much the same, and Englishmen enjoyed many of the activities that still have a place in their recreations. To have an understanding of the social life and customs of a nation, a knowledge of its recreations is essential. The way a people spend their moments of leisure provides a clue to their personalities and qualities of character.

During the years when the Tudors and early Stuarts governed England, roads were poor, travel was difficult and sometimes dangerous, and ordinary folk usually did not go far beyond their parish limits for pleasure. Furthermore, life was hard for the ordinary citizen, and few had time for much leisure. Consequently, both time and opportunity were lacking for organized sports that could attract widespread attendance like a modern football match or modern horse racing. To working men and apprentices many sports were forbidden by statute except on such specified holidays as Christmas, but the laws were not always rigidly enforced.

Despite difficulties and handicaps, however, people of all classes enjoyed a variety of simple sports and amusements. If the Elizabethans had to work long hours at hard tasks, they nevertheless found time for play and gaiety. Fairs, festivals, and church wakes provided opportunities to villagers for many amusements. Everyone could look forward to the local fair, at which vendors of a variety of wares spread out their goods for sale. To the fairs came gleemen, jugglers, tumblers, acrobats, and animal trainers with their beasts: a dancing bear, monkeys, an exotic camel, and an "educated" horse. Traveling showmen also brought freaks, as in the "sideshow" at carnivals today, and sleight-of-hand artists were common. After the buying and selling were over, visitors to the fair, adults and children alike, joined in the activities. Women might dance for a prize, and the men engaged in foot races, bowling matches, wrestling, and other similar competitions. One of the most curious events, at which stout young men sought to show their worth and endurance, was the sport of shin kicking. Before this event the participants rubbed both their boots and shins with blue vitriol to harden them. At the close of the day many a young countryman must have been sore and sorry.

Festivals celebrated special occasions, such as the end of the harvest, sheepshearing, and the beginning of spring. Church wakes were held on a saint's day or the day of dedication of the church. A wake began with the vigil at the church and a service; then followed feasting, drinking, and contests of skill and strength like those at fairs. Originally these celebrations were held in the churchyard, but as the activities became more and more secular the churchyard was abandoned or forbidden. Many of the festivals stemmed from pagan rites, and the church thought to remove the taint of heathenism somewhat by acknowledging and modifying them. With the rise of the Puritans, however, objections grew louder, especially to such celebrations as church ales. On these occasions the churchwardens provided a quantity of malt, some from the church stock and the rest from parishioners. The malt was brewed into beer and ale and then sold to raise money for the church. This practice was condemned vociferously by Philip Stubbes, who complained in his *Anatomy of Abuses* (1583) of a situation in which profit to the church increased in proportion to the consumption of beer and the drunkenness that followed.

Pious Philip Stubbes also spoke out against the revelry that took place on May Day. On the eve of this holiday, or in the early morning hours of the day itself, people were accustomed to go into the forests to gather boughs and branches as decorations for their homes. A Maypole would be cut and drawn into the village by oxen. Each ox had flowers tied to its horns and

2

the pole was decorated with herbs, flowers, and ribbons. When the pole was erected, the dancing began. The morris dance was traditional on May Day with a fiddler, Maid Marian, and ten men dressed with horns and bells. Maid Marian was queen of the May and mistress of the archery games. In later years Robin Hood was introduced, probably as king of the May. Upon such levity Stubbes frowned, but he deplored most the fact that the young men and girls "run gadding over night to the woods, groves, hills, and mountains" and there spend the night "in pleasant pastimes." He declared on "good authority" (one wonders if his own) that of a hundred maids going out scarcely a third returned in the state of virginity.

Archery occupied an important place in the May-Day activities, for it was virtually the national sport. Laws discouraged other physical exercises so that men would not be diverted from the practice of archery. From the time of Edward III when the value of the longbow was effectively demonstrated, it was thought wise to have all the men of England ready as trained archers in case of war. By the beginning of the seventeenth century the usefulness of archery in war was declining. As R. Barret says in *The Theory and Practice of Modern Wars* (1598) "they [archers] may serve to some sorts of service, but to no such effect as any of the fiery weapons," but the victories of the longbow at Crécy, Poitiers, and Agincourt were not quickly forgotten, and every man was expected to own a longbow and to practice regularly. Shooting contests were held to stimulate interest, and even churchwardens' accounts sometimes include expenses for making archery butts. Butts were mounds of earth, banked with turf. Against this mound was placed a white disk for a target. Shooting at these taught accuracy. To learn to "keep a length" the archers practiced "prick" or "clout" shooting, which meant shooting at a target eighteen inches in diameter, stuffed with straw. This mark was placed at a distance of 160 to 240 yards. "Roving" was to shoot in the open, at no mark, and at unknown distances.

Archery was praised as good for all men, great or poor. Gervase Markham in *The Art of Archery* (1634), dedicated to

Illus. 1. Morris dancers. Engraving by I. Jones [n.d.]
in the Folger Library.

Charles I, calls it an honest and wholesome sport, and much earlier, in *Toxophilus* (1545), Roger Ascham referred to archery as "the most honest pastime of all" and a cure of evil gaming. Ascham, who was at one time tutor to Elizabeth I, felt that a genuine effort should be made to teach archery because, truth to tell, the interest in archery was waning. He felt that many disobeyed the royal laws for lack of knowledge of how to shoot. Christina Hole suggests in *English Sports and Pastimes* that enthusiasm died out because laws commanded the practice of archery instead of leaving it to the pleasure of sportsmen.

An act passed in 1541 in the reign of Henry VIII shows us to what extent the government favored archery. After declaring that all able men under sixty must own a longbow and practice shooting, the act continues with a list of activities which are banned: "That no manner of person or persons . . . shall for his or their gain . . . keep . . . or maintain, any common house, alley, or place of bowling, quoiting, cloish, kayles, half-bowl, tennis, dicing, table, or carding, or any other manner of game prohibited by any statute heretofore made, or any unlawful new game now invented or made, or any other new unlawful game hereafter to be invented, found, had or made. . . ."

In spite of this act gaming houses were kept open, and the various sports flourished. Bowling was probably the most popular. Robert Crowley, printer and Puritan preacher as well as poet, testifies that bowling was not suppressed. In his *One and Thirty Epigrams* (1550), appeared this poem on bowling:

> Two sorts of alleys
> In London I find;
> The one against the law,
> And the other against kind.
> The first is where bowling
> Forbidden, men use,
> And wasting their goods,
> Do their labor refuse.
> But in London (alas!)
> Some men are devilishly
> Suffered to profess it
> As an art to live by. . . .

5

Two types of bowling were popular then as now. The favorite was played on bowling greens. Bowling in alleys, similar to the modern game, was also common. Bowling greens were often included as part of the gardens in the estates of the gentry, but bowling was not a sport for the rich alone. Besides having alleys in the supposedly illegal gaming houses, men also played at bowls in the open country, according to Gervase Markham's description in *Country Contentments* (1615): "There is another recreation . . . that is, bowling, in which a man shall find great art in choosing out his ground and preventing the winding, hanging, and many turning advantages of the same, whether it be in open wild places or in close alleys; and in this sport the choosing of the bowl is the greatest cunning; your flat bowls being the best for alleys, your round biased bowls for open grounds of advantage, and your round bowls like a ball for greenswards that are plain and level." Charles Cotton, who in the later seventeenth century wrote *The Complete Gamester* (1674), "borrowed" this passage from Markham. Cotton, however, does add a caution against gambling at a bowling match. In his advice on learning the game he states that "practice must be your best tutor . . . ; all that I shall say, have a care you are not in the first place rooked out of your money." Cotton's comments on the weird postures assumed by bowlers as the bowl is rolling down the alley, and the cries to go further or stop shorter, suggest that a bowler of the sixteenth century would not feel out of place in a twentieth-century bowling alley.

Many of the bowling terms, such as "rub," "jack," or "kiss," can be found in Shakespeare, and it appears probable that he was a knowledgeable bowler. A "rub" is anything that diverts the ball from its course (as in Hamlet's soliloquy: "Ay, there's the rub"); a "jack" (also "master" or "mistress") is a small bowl placed as a mark at which to aim; and a "kiss" occurs when one bowl touches another (as in *Cymbeline*, II.i.: "Was there ever man had such luck! When I kissed the jack, upon an up-cast to be hit away!").

Kayles, cloish, and loggats were all closely allied to bowling. In the game of kayles there were six or more pins set up in a straight row. Instead of bowling a ball at the pins, the object

Illus. 2. Football. From Henry Peacham, *Minerva Britanna* (1612).

Illus. 3. Bowling. From *Le centre de l'amour* [1650?].

was to knock the pins down by throwing a stick at them. Cloish also consisted of setting pins in a row, but a bowl was used to knock them down. In loggats, a game popular with boys and country folk, bones were substituted for the pins, and another bone was thrown at them. Shakespeare has a reference to this sport in the grave-digging scene where Hamlet comments: "Did these bones cost no more the breeding but to play at loggats with 'em?"

Men and boys of the sixteenth century, like their counterparts in other ages, enjoyed various forms of ball games. The variety of games played with balls was great, but often the same game appeared in different sections of the country under different names. As early as 1598 one finds a reference to cricket being played fifty years before. Cricket perhaps was an outgrowth of stoolball and clubball. In playing stoolball, a bowler tried to hit a stool with a ball. One player tried to defend the stool with his hand. In some localities a bat was used. In this game, however, there were no runs. Another game with overtones of cricket was trapball. A ball was placed in a spoon-shaped piece of wood. When the spoon was hit, the ball would rise and was hit into the field. Opponents tried to catch the ball, or to bowl the ball in to hit the trap.

Handball is probably the oldest form of ball game. Many games were derived from it, including fives and a form of tennis. Fives was played against a wall or church tower. This led to complaints from ministers against the delinquent boys who not only did not attend church but disturbed the service by playing ball against the church walls! Rules apparently differed in various geographical areas, as at Eton, where the buttresses from the wall formed two additional sides, and the game called "Eton Fives" developed.

Football was not unknown to the Elizabethan age, but it is hardly recognizable as the game we know today. The main similarity is that a ball, usually a bladder filled with air and encased in leather, was used, and the object was to get the ball across a goal line. What happened in between was nothing short of chaos or, as Sir Thomas Elyot says in *The Book Named the*

Illus. 4. Balloon ball and wrestling in the foreground, with other activities in the background. From Erasmo di Valvasone, *La caccia* [1602].

Governor (1531), "nothing but beastly fury and extreme violence." There were few if any rules, and each team could have an unlimited number of players. Often there were interparish contests, in which case much of the parish might be commandeered for the playing field, as one set of players tried to kick the ball into the opposing parish. On other occasions an open field or common was used. If the game was a parish affair, it was usually played on a holiday or feast day. At Chester a game was always played at Shrovetide, and legend has it that it commemorated the kicking about of the head of a captured Dane. Often it was a contest between two special groups of people, such as married men and bachelors. At Inverness, Scotland, an annual game was played between the married and the single women—and it is reported that the married women usually won!

Football was another sport prohibited by law to the working man as early as 1349 and as late as Elizabeth's reign. James I in *Basilicon Doron* (1599), a book of instructions for his son, forbids the prince to play football because he thought it "meeter for laming than making able the users thereof." Philip Stubbes gives us a vivid description in his *Anatomy of Abuses* of what happens during a game which he considers a "bloody and murdering practice."

For doth not everyone lie in wait for his adversary, seeking to overthrow him and to pick him on his nose, though it be upon hard stones, in ditch or dale, in valley or hill . . . he careth not so he have him down . . . so that by this means, sometimes their necks are broken, sometimes their backs . . . legs . . . arms. . . .

. . . They have the sleights to meet one betwixt two, to dash him against the heart with their elbows, to hit him under the shortribs with their gripped fists, and with their knees to catch him upon the hip and to pick him on his neck, with a hundred such murdering devices. . . .

Such a commentary suggests that Stubbes himself had been involved at least once in a friendly game of football.

Robert Burton in his *Anatomy of Melancholy* (1621) enu-

Illus. 5. Frontispiece to Matthew Walbancke's *Annalia Dubrensia* (1636), show-ing some of the activities of the Cotswold Games.

merates additional sports enjoyed by country folk and working people. They include quoits (similar to throwing horseshoes), pitching bars, hurling, wrestling (best done by those who knew the Cornish hug), leaping, running, fencing, swimming, football, balloon, and quintain. Balloon ball was, according to Markham's *Country Contentments*, "a strong and moving sport in the open fields, with a great ball of double leather filled with wind, and driven to and fro with the strength of a man's arm armed in a bracer of wood, either of which actions must be learned by the eye and practice." Quintain was at one time a knightly exercise. In the late sixteenth century it became a rustic pastime. The quintain was a post with a swinging shield attached. The object was to rush at the shield as if in a duel and then quickly to maneuver oneself out of the way as the shield swung around the post. The slow-footed were hit in the back of the head by the returning shield.

In the reign of James I the celebrated Cotswold Games, which exemplified many of the popular recreations of the day, grew into national importance. These games had begun in the reign of Elizabeth I, or perhaps even earlier, as a small local gathering, but they were taken over in the next reign by a man who had many of the qualities of a modern promoter, a certain "Captain" Robert Dover, who obtained from King James a royal sanction for the games and received from His Majesty as a further token of favor an old hat, a feather, and a ruff, which he wore with great pride. Information about the Cotswold Games is to be found in *Annalia Dubrensia* (1636), a volume edited by Matthew Walbancke, containing poems by Michael Drayton, Ben Jonson, and others in praise of Captain Dover and his activities. The Cotswold Games were compared by some to those held in classical times on Mt. Olympus. One poem by William Denny mentions foot racing, wrestling, bowling, chariot races, coursing with greyhounds, leaping, and throwing the sledge. Inside tents one could play chess; Irish, which resembles backgammon; and cent, a card game. Other activities included dancing and horse racing.

Elizabethan children had many ways of amusing themselves,

Illus. 6. Children's games including whipping the top, marbles, and walking on stilts. From Jacob Cats, *Silenus Alcibiadis* (1622).

and some of their games are still familiar to juveniles. It would be impossible to list all the games at which children played, but a few will illustrate their characteristic amusements: put-die, blind egg, conquers, hoodman-blind, nine-men's morris, and top and scourge. Dice were needed to play put-die. Instead of numbers there were letters on each die—P, T, H, and L on the four sides, and A and D on the two ends. The dice were tossed in the air. Whatever letter turned up determined the number of marbles won or lost from the pool. Blind egg consisted of lining birds' eggs in a row. A blindfolded boy then tried to break the eggs with a stick. In one version of conquers the players took snail shells and pressed them together. The one whose shell did not break was the winner. Hoodman-blind, of course, is simply a variant form of blindman's buff. Nine-men's morris went by several names, one of which was merels. In this game each player had nine wooden pegs. A flat board with three squares and twenty-four holes was used, and the object was to capture the opponent's pegs and to get one's own pegs in three straight rows. This game was also played outdoors, using the ground for a board. Top and scourge was a seasonal game, connected with the Lenten season, in which a boy would whip a top to make it spin.

Recreation was obviously not restricted to any age group or class. Although the lower classes had certain handicaps, they found numerous ways of amusing themselves. The gentry and nobility naturally had few restrictions upon their recreations. Indeed, an ability in sports was an essential requirement for a young gentleman. One of the most noted books of instructions to young men of gentle breeding is Baldassare Castiglione's *The Courtier*, translated into English by Thomas Hoby in 1561. In this conduct book Castiglione lists among the chief qualifications of a courtier skill in martial exercises and in sports. The courtier must be able to fence with all kinds of weapons, to play tennis, to hunt, to hawk, and to ride well. Other activities suitable for young aristocrats were swimming, leaping, vaulting, wrestling, and casting stones or an iron bar. Here Castiglione gives an admonition "not to run, wrestle, leap, or cast the stone

14

Illus. 7. Swimming. From Everard Digby, *De arte natandi* (1587).

or bar with men of the country, except he be sure to get the victory." It was not fitting for a gentleman to lose to someone of baser birth, and gentlemen engaged in these sports either alone or with their equals. On the other hand, one could tilt, ride in a tourney, and throw the spear or dart in public to delight the common people. Nicholas Faret in *The Honest Man,* translated by Edward Grimstone in 1632, gives virtually the same qualifications for proper gentlemanly behavior. Besides the foregoing skills a courtier was expected to have some knowledge of music and be able to play the lute or gittern and to carry a fair tune.

A courtier's life was devoted to following his prince, a life that provided in the Tudor age ample opportunity for a high-spirited young gentleman to develop his love of martial exercises. Henry VIII was fond of these sports and in his reign they flourished. Edward Hall's *Chronicle,* first published in 1548, describes the King's activities while on progress. Henry exercised himself with shooting, singing, dancing, wrestling, casting of the bar, jousts and tourneys, hunting and hawking. At times the King and another would issue a challenge to others to take part in some martial activity. On one occasion Henry and the Duke of Suffolk "were defenders at the tilt against all comers." Another time the King and two aides challenged all to fight "at the barriers with target and casting the spear of eight feet long." Then they challenged all to fight them for seven strokes with two-handed swords. To encourage further these manly sports, the King had built at Greenwich a place for the ladies to watch fights with battle-axes, because, Hall says, "the King [was] not minded to see young gentlemen unexpert in martial feats." To keep fit for these activities a man needed practice, and several hours a day might be devoted to riding at the tilt or ring. To tilt was to ride with a lance at a mark, or quintain. Although this later became a rustic pastime, it served as good exercise for aspiring knights. Another exercise was to ride with spear or lance and try to catch a ring hung from a pole, a feat that has survived to modern times.

Fencing became exceedingly popular in the reign of Henry

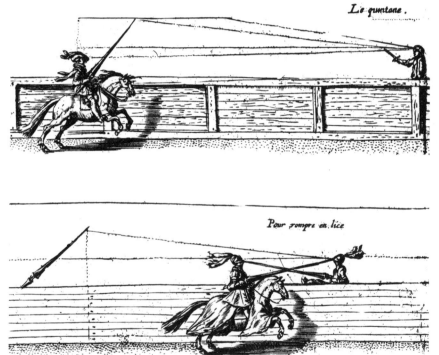

Illus. 8. Running at the quintain and jousting. From Antoine de Pluvinel, *L'instruction du roy* (1627).

Illus. 9. Tripping up the opponent. From Camillo Agrippa, *Trattato di scienza d'arme* (1568).

VIII, in part as a result of the King's own interest. By letters patent Henry VIII gave to the Masters of Defense a monopoly of teaching arms. In earlier years all free Englishmen carried arms, but fencing was looked down upon as being too subtle an activity and one that took away from true valor. To the medieval mind plain and simple hacking from left to right with sword and buckler was the mark of a man. It took some time for the English to learn new tactics and change their way of thinking. The gradual change was due largely to the Italian masters of arms who braved English criticism to teach their modern methods. The art of fencing developed in Italy, and Italian methods were far ahead of the English. The Italians discarded the buckler and added the poniard to the left hand. The poniard itself was finally discarded, and the sword was thenceforth used for both offense and defense. The "point" of the sword was rediscovered, and fencers learned the advantage of the thrust, called *stoccata* by the Italian fencing masters, over the side blows. In English tradition the use of the point was originally considered a dishonor.

In Elizabeth's reign the court went through an Italianate period, at which time the rapier was adopted. John Florio, an Italian naturalized in England, wrote in his *First Fruits* (1578) of the sword and buckler as "a clownish and dastardly weapon, and none for a gentleman." On the other hand, George Silver, an ardent Englishman, vigorously defended the short sword against the rapier and warned against Italian and other foreign methods. Shakespeare showed himself a loyal Englishman by satirizing the Italianate form of fencing in his plays. Silver practiced what he preached, for he was unaware of the lunge which was then being taught in Italy. His method of attack was to jump forward with both feet. He also advocated disarming and tripping, which apparently was not unsportsmanlike; at any rate, Castiglione recommended wrestling to young gentlemen because it was useful in the handling of weapons on foot. The rapier survived the Italianate period and passed on down to the middle class, and many Englishmen, despite Silver's warning, came to recognize it as a fine weapon. Joseph Swetnam, for ex-

ample, in his *School of the Noble . . . Science of Defense* (1616)
considered rapiers as the "finest and most comeliest weapons
that were used in England. The short sword against the rapier
is little better than a tobacco-pipe."

By 1639 a book called *Pallas Armata*, by G. A., introduced
new methods of fencing which were the forerunners of present-
day fencing techniques. The author advocates the single sword
or single rapier. The dagger, gauntlet, and buckler (formerly
used in the left hand as a means of defense) were no longer
considered fashionable.

For townspeople in this period one of the most popular spec-
tacles was "playing a prize." To become a master of arms, the
aspirant had to challenge all masters within a certain radius.
These contests were held in public and were preceded by a
march through the town with drums to announce the coming
event. Municipal authorities usually frowned on these events
and often refused to give licenses, but outside the town
boundaries contestants could find places for these competitions.
Although blunted swords were used, the battles were lusty and
long. In fact they were as much a contest of endurance as of
skill, for the challenger had to fight each master with a certain
number of weapons for a prescribed length of time. Between
each event the challenger would parade around and exhort the
crowd to contribute money, for that is how he paid all his expenses. The weapons in which a master of arms had to be pro-
ficient were the two-handed sword, hand-and-one-half sword,
long sword, backsword, sword and buckler, sword and dagger,
pike, morris- or half-pike, halberd, quarterstaff, and battle-axe.
By 1605 most of these weapons were obsolete, but the English
teachers of arms clung tenaciously to all of them for many years.

A princely sport and one enjoyed by all the sovereigns of the
age was hunting. Deer, hare, and otter were the principal quar-
ries. Boars were hunted to a lesser degree than on the Continent because they were not so prevalent in England. Boar
hunting was a dangerous sport not only to the hunter but to his
hounds. Although the English loved the chase, English hunting
books for the most part followed the French originals, and the

Illus. 10. Queen Elizabeth being offered the knife to slit the throat of the slain deer. From George Turberville, *The Noble Art of Venery* [1575].

Illus. 11. Hunting the deer with hounds. From George Turberville, *The Noble Art of Venery* [1575].

customs were largely of French derivation. George Turberville in his *Noble Art of Venery or Hunting*, first printed about 1576, took much of his material directly from *La Venerie de Jacques du Fouilloux* and some from Gaston Phoebus. The English did not always observe fixed rules, but there was a certain pattern or ritual in their procedures, particularly in deer hunting.

This sport was engaged in not only for pleasure's sake, but for necessity as well. Killing a deer meant good meat, much needed in the winter, and therefore the choice of the deer was important. Before the hunt began huntsmen would go out early to locate a hart which would be good for hunting. There were many ways of doing this. A good huntsman would judge the age and size of the hart by the shape of the slots, or footprints. The droppings or "fewmets" provided other evidence of the age and state of the animal. The size of the animal's head and body could be guessed by the height and width of the space between twigs broken in passing. A huntsman would judge the hart's gait to see how long it could last in a chase; it was desirable to find a fat animal that would tire in a reasonable time. All of these signs might not be detectable on one hunting expedition but such information as a huntsman could gather was delivered to the prince or the master of game, who would then decide which animal was to be hunted.

After the deer was aroused from his lair, the chase was on. Old experienced hounds were the best, for they did not easily lose the scent. If the chase was a long one, the hounds were sent in in relays; that is, fresh hounds were brought in at intervals to continue the hunt. When the hart was caught, it was skinned and butchered immediately. Certain portions were given to special people: the participants of noblest birth and the huntsman in charge; even the hounds were allowed their bit. It was the prerogative of the prince to slit the throat and cut off the head. Often chafing dishes, coals, sauces, spices, and wines were brought along to heat and cook some of the delicacies, "caul, tongue, ears, doucets, tenderlings," reserved for the prince. Wine was also brought along for another purpose, for there was a superstition that the huntsman must take a drink of wine before breaking up the deer or the venison would putrify and stink.

When men wanted to exercise their cunning, show off the speed of their hounds, and pursue the chase for sheer pleasure, they usually chose the hare, for the hare was the swiftest of creatures. Sir Thomas Elyot in *The Book Named the Governor* commends this sport as suitable for scholars and women: "Hunting of the hare with greyhounds is a right good solace for men that be studious, or them to whom nature hath not given personage or courage apt for the wars. Also for gentlewomen which fear neither sun nor wind for appairing their beauty."

Although there were no hunting seasons such as we observe in this century, George Turberville recommends October and November as the best months, for in the summer the heat would be too great for the hounds, and in the spring the smell of the flowers and herbs would make them lose their scent.

In hunting otter a special spear or forked staff was used. The hounds would smell out the otter, but it was the huntsman's job to catch him if he went to the river. In this case a man would stand on each side of the river holding a line stretched across the stream. The line would be held slack so that it would sink under the water. The direction and whereabouts of the otter could be determined when it hit the line.

When boar hunting, Turberville suggests that dogs wear bells around their necks, for the boar will be frightened by the sound of bells and will flee instead of standing at bay or charging. Whether this was true or not, it was certainly wise to use the most experienced hounds in this dangerous sport. As in hunting a deer, the size of the boar could first be determined by his tracks or by seeing where he had rooted in a hedge. Another way was to find where the boar had rubbed against a tree after rolling in the mud. The weapon used in this sport was a long spear with a crosspiece. The crossbar was to prevent the spear from sticking too far into the boar as he charged against it.

Fox hunting as it is known today did not develop fully until the late seventeenth or early eighteenth century. Foxes as well

Illus. *12.* Boar hunting with a spear
with a crossbar. From Guillaume de La
Perrière, *La morosophie* (1553).

as badgers were hunted as vermin and were dug out of their dens and killed. Terriers held the foxes or badgers in their burrows while the huntsman with spade or mattock dug them out. In addition to a supply of food and drink, Turberville advises a stout pair of boots, for, he laments, "I have lent a fox or a badger ere now, a piece of my hose, and the skin and flesh for company, which he never restored again." A hunt might last a long time, and Turberville recommends that a gentleman take along several mats to lie upon the ground. In some cases they even used inflated mattresses or "a windbed which is made of leather strongly sewn on all the four sides, and having a pipe at one of the corners to blow it as you would blow a bagpipe, and when it is blown full of wind, to stop it up and lie upon it on the ground."

Falcons were used for hunting of fowl and some game. Hawking, one of the oldest sports known, was expensive and therefore restricted to the aristocracy; it was greatly favored by the English nobility and gentry. Certain laws indicate the esteem in which falconry was held. One law stated that a lost hawk must be returned, or the finder would be charged with a felony, as would the stealer of a hawk's eggs. James I passed a law forbidding the shooting of game by guns, crossbows, or longbows, except to kill crows or smaller birds to feed the hawks. This is probably not so much an indication of James' love of hawking as it is an indication of his upbringing in Scotland, where shooting with gun and bow was considered thievish. James praised hawking sparingly in *Basilicon Doron* and thought that for Prince Henry hunting with hounds was better than hunting with hawks. Falconry is uncertain and more apt to stir up the emotions, the King observed.

The training of a hawk required patience and gentleness, but first a proper hawk had to be caught. Sometimes they were taken while they were just learning to hop from branch to branch, in which case they were known as branches. A soar hawk was taken wild in its first year, and an eyas was taken from the nest. Immediately after the hawks were caught, jesses, which were straps of leather, were attached to their feet and

Illus. 13. Hawking. From Erasmo di Valvasone, *La caccia* [1602].

never removed. Rings of silver called vervels, to which the jesses were attached, were also put around the legs. Preparatory to training was seeling, in which a thread was drawn through the eyelids so that the eyes were partially closed to keep out daylight. This was supposed to help the hawk become adjusted to wearing a hood, which completely covered the head. A hawk was kept with a sharp appetite so as to respond to the bits fed her by the falconer. When the hawk learned to jump from the perch to the fist and to respond to the trainer's voice, it could be taught to come to the lure. The lure was a piece of meat, often a dead pigeon, used to get the falcon back to the owner. If a hawk remained wild and would not submit to training, then it was kept awake until fatigue tamed it.

There are many kinds of hawks, each with their special virtues, but they fall into two general classes: short-winged and long-winged hawks. The goshawk and sparrow hawk are short-winged and were used in woody areas or among shrubs. These hawks were flown from the hand, and they killed their prey on the ground with their beaks. Long-winged hawks include the gerfalcon, falcon, lanner, merlin, hobby, and kestrel. They were used in the open country. A hawk would hover above the falconer until the dogs stirred up the game, at which time the falcon would swoop down and kill its quarry in the air with a stroke of the claw. These hawks were brought back by the lure, and when flying they had bells attached to their legs so that the owner could find them again.

Fowling was popular with those people to whom hawking was denied because of class, time, or money. Since the Elizabethans, like many modern Europeans, enjoyed eating a variety of birds large and small, fowling was pursued primarily for food. Though some of the methods used to secure birds for the pot were ingenious and skillful, they were hardly sportsmanlike in the usual sense. Nets and snares of various kinds were common devices for catching birds. A snare of the springe type—a noose tied to the end of a pliant rod and triggered to tighten up when touched—was one of the most common. Also used were traps known as pitfalls.

Illus. 14. Falcons attacking in flight. From George Turberville, *The Book of Falconry* (1575).

Illus. 15. Fowling. From Johann Mannich, *Sacra emblemata* (1624–25).

Illus. 16. Fishing. From Levinus Hulsius, *De quadrante geometrico* (1594).

Birdliming was another ingenious way of catching small birds. Small twigs from a willow were covered with birdlime, a sticky substance, and were scattered about a stale, or decoy. When the birds settled onto these twigs, they were unable to free themselves and the fowler could gather them in at his leisure. Dogs were sometimes used to retrieve any who managed to get loose; such dogs were trained to lie nearby and snatch up any bird which struggled free before it could fly away.

Somewhat more sport was involved in shooting birds, which was done with bird bolts (arrows with blunt heads) or stonebows (catapults which shot small pebbles). Firearms were beginning to come into use but were too clumsy as yet for shooting any but large game birds. Because birds are easily frightened, it was desirable to take them by surprise, and for this purpose a stalking-horse was used. This was originally a real cow, ox, or horse which had been trained to walk gently back and forth, while behind it the hunter drew a bead on his quarry. Dummy animals made of wood and canvas were also used in lieu of the living specimens. Even King Henry VIII used this method of hunting.

Fowling at night required different techniques—the two most popular being "lowbelling" and "batfowling." In the former the hunter carried a bell with a low, hollow sound which caused the birds to lie close. A large net was spread and then the birds were stirred up and caught in the net. Batfowling was a procedure in which the birds were confused by fires set in iron vessels. When the birds were caught in the light of the fires, they were batted down with broomlike poles.

Fishing was as popular with Tudor Englishmen as it is with men of the atomic age. These fishermen of old had just as much trouble catching fish as men of all centuries, although modern editors of Elizabethan fishing treatises contend that fish have grown craftier over the years. Methods and equipment were somewhat different then. Although fishing rods could be bought at the haberdasher's, the various books on the subject describe the rod and line with such care that it is evident that many Elizabethans were given to making their own. Rods were of three types, according to Markham's *Pleasures of Princes* (1614): of two pieces, the lower being nine to ten feet and the upper about a yard long; of one whole piece, which meant a short rod good only for narrow streams; of many pieces, usually made of cane, that fit into one another. The line was made of horsehair with threads of silk intertwined. Some years later Robert Venables in *The Experienced Angler* (1662) preferred a line of either horsehair or silk, but not a mixture.

Until the middle of the seventeenth century fishermen had no reels. Since the line was attached to a loop at the end of the rod, it was not possible to play the trout until it tired. Even when reels did appear, they were used more for salmon than for trout.

Elizabethan fishermen did not favor fishing upstream with a dry fly. Upstream angling was first mentioned by Venables and then with disapproval. He believed that in casting upstream one's line was more likely to hit the water before the fly, or at least the line would be visible, and in either case the fish would be frightened away—all of which argues the inexpertness of Venables as a fly-caster or the poor quality of the equipment then available.

Various baits were used, and Venables suggests that once a week a fisherman, if he had a special fishing spot, should cast in all sort of food, such as corn boiled soft, grain dipped in blood, or worms. Then the fish would be less suspicious of bait. Live baits consisted of such delicacies as red worms, maggots, flies, grasshoppers, hornets, wasps, and snails. Dried wasps, clotted blood of sheep, corn, seed, cheese, berries, cherries, or pastes were used as dead bait. For those who preferred fly-fishing, books told how to make one's own flies. According to Izaak Walton's classic, *The Compleat Angler*, "if he hit to make his fly right, and have the luck to hit, also, where there is store of trouts, a dark day, and a right wind, he will catch such store of them as will encourage him to grow more and more in love with the art of fly-making." This implies a big "if," but all writers on fishing stress the virtues a fisherman must have, the foremost being patience. As Markham writes: "Then he must be exceeding patient and neither vex nor excruciate himself with losses or mischances, as in losing the prey when it is almost in the hand, or by breaking his tools."

One unusual form of fishing was "tickling," in which a fisherman cautiously ran his arm under a bank until he touched a trout and then slowly tickled it until he was in a position to seize it.

Fishing was a sport sufficiently in favor to receive the blessing of university authorities in a day when sports had only a small place in university life. Sir Simonds D'Ewes mentions in a diary kept at Cambridge that angling was one of the pleasures that he enjoyed. D'Ewes also mentions a few other sports which served "as antidotes to disastrous diseases" and of course did not interfere with studies, unlike the experience of Sir Andrew Aguecheek in *Twelfth Night*, who laments: "I would I had bestowed that time in the tongues that I have in fencing, dancing, and bearbaiting."

Sports in which the students participated in their leisure time included tennis, shovegroat (shuffleboard), cards, bowling, jumping, and running. They seem to agree with Robert Crowley's idea of how a scholar should amuse himself.

> To fish, to fowl, to hunt, to hawk,
> Or on an instrument to play;
> And some whiles to commune and talk,
> No man is able to gainsay.
> To shoot, to bowl, or cast the bar,
> To play tennis, or toss the ball
> Or to run base, like men of war,
> Shall hurt thy study nought at all.
> For all these things do recreate,
> The mind, if thou canst hold the mean.

Scottish universities, somewhat more advanced than those below the border, included sports and exercises as a part of the official curriculum. On certain days the students were taken to the fields for organized exercises, and the University of Edinburgh had a tennis court on its grounds. James Melville, whose memoirs

33

Illus. 17. A game of tennis. From *Le centre de l'amour* [1650?].

dating from the late sixteenth century were published in 1842, states that at school he was taught archery, golf, fencing, running, leaping, and wrestling, and at the University of St. Andrews he played golf and engaged in archery.

Golf was a great recreation in Scotland from early times, though it did not thrive in England until the Stuart kings popularized it there. The treasurer's records in the reign of James IV of Scotland included expenses for golf equipment:

1503, Feb. 3.   Item to the King to play at the
golf with the Earl of Bothwell . . . . xlii s
1503, Feb. 4.   Item to golf clubs and balls
to the King . . . . ix s
1503, Feb. 22.   Item, xii golf balls to the King . . . . iiii s
1506,   Item the 28th day of July for ii golf
clubs to the King . . . . ii s

Golf balls at this time were stuffed with feathers and covered with leather.

Tennis was played in both England and Scotland as well as on the Continent. In fact, it developed from the French *jeu de paume* or "palm play." In its early stages in the Middle Ages the palm of the hand was used instead of a racket. The hand was gloved, and later strings were stretched between the fingers of the glove. The next step was a crude racket with a handle. For a long time both the hand and the racket were used, but the racket had become sufficiently popular by Chaucer's day to be mentioned in his *Troilus and Criseyde*. The racket was oblong and strung diagonally with only a few strings.

The common people played some form of open-air tennis, but the game was largely the court tennis variety, played in an enclosed court. Because of the expense it was confined for the most part to the gentry and nobility, who could afford to build their own courts. Some public courts, however, were operated by the proprietors of gaming houses.

The actual size of the courts varied, but they all had the same features: the outer and inner walls, covered by a sloping roof called the penthouse; the dedans, a large opening at the end of the service side of the court; the grille, a small opening in the end corner of the hazard side; galleries along the side; and the lines in the court by which to mark a chase.

The object was to hit the ball back and forth, sometimes with the aid of the walls, until a point was won or lost, or a chase was made. A chase occurred when one player elected not to hit the ball, but to let it fall. Where it fell was marked, and the players changed sides, giving the opponent an opportunity to make a better chase—one that was further from the net. A point also was won if the ball was struck through the dedans or grille.

Tennis balls in the sixteenth century were stuffed with feathers or hair and encased in white leather. This made them stronger and more resilient than the earlier cloth balls. That hair was a popular stuffing is indicated by the many references to it in contemporary literature as in *Much Ado About Nothing*, III.ii:

> *Don Pedro.* Hath any man seen him at the barber's?
> *Claudio.* No, but the barber's man hath been seen with him, and the old ornament of his cheeks hath already stuffed tennis balls.

Tennis was a popular game with royalty. Most of the royal palaces had courts. Henry VII and his son Henry VIII were enthusiastic players, and Elizabeth apparently enjoyed the game, for there are reports of special games being played for her amusement while on progresses. The Stuart kings also regarded tennis with favor, and James I in *Basilicon Doron* included it in the list of approved sports for Prince Henry.

Proof that tennis was a gentleman's game is found in John Earle's *Microcosmography* (1628), where the character of a gentleman at the university is described thus: "The two marks of his seniority is the bare velvet of his gown and his proficiency at tennis, where when he can once play a set he is a freshman no more."

In a country of inclement weather indoor games were bound to be popular. Furthermore, even the most active could not always be running, leaping, or hitting balls, and there are always those who have no desire to engage in active sports. For moments of less activity there were cards and table games. The origin of card games dates far back in history. Cardplaying had spread over Europe before it crossed the Channel into England. By the fifteenth century card games were common in England, and Edward IV in 1463 forbade the importation of playing cards to protect local cardmakers. By 1496 cardplaying was added to the list of activities forbidden the laboring classes. Henry VII's law read that servants and apprentices could play at cards only during the Christmas holiday, and then only in their master's house. In 1628 a charter was granted the London Company of Makers of Playing Cards.

It is uncertain whether English cards were derived more from French or Spanish cards. They appear to have taken the names of their suits and the symbols from both. The Spanish suits were *espadas* (swords), *copas* (cups), *dineros* (coins), and *bastos* (clubs). In France the suits were *piques* (spears), *coeurs* (hearts), *carreaux* (squares or lozenges), and *trefles* (trefoils). The face cards on French cards were named after various emperors, queens, or famous knights. The knaves appeared in various dress, including armor, depending on the current events of a particular period. Samuel Rowlands in 1612, in his *Knave of Hearts*, indicated that the English jacks were dressed in the costume of Chaucer's time.

> We are abused in a great degree;
> For, there's no knaves so wronged as are we
> By those that chiefly should be our part-takers:
> And thus it is my masters, you cardmakers.
> All other knaves are at their own free will,
> To brave it out, and follow fashion still
> In any cut, according to the time:
> But we poor knaves (I know not for what crime)
> Are kept in piebald suits which we have worn
> Hundred of years; this hardly can be borne.
> The idle-headed French devised us first,
> Who of all fashion-mongers is the worst.

Illus. 18. Playing at cards. From Johan de Brune, *Emblemata* (1624).

Cardplaying, as well as dicing, was condemned by many. Some claimed it to be an invention of the Devil, and because the cards were named, they described cardplaying as a form of idolatry. John Northbrooke in his *Treatise wherein Dicing, Dancing . . . Are Reproved,* published about 1577, felt that cardplaying was not so evil as dicing because there was less trust in chance. But since cardplaying furnished small training for the mind, he saw little good in it. According to him, cheating was prevalent, "either by pricking of a card, or pinching of it, cutting at the nick; either by a bum-card [i.e., a raised or marked card for cheating] finely, under, over, or in the middle, &c. and what not to deceive?" Although moralists condemned cardplaying and rogues cheated, the various games remained extremely popular through the years. Primero was played by Elizabeth I. It was a game at which two or three could play. In this the ace of spades was the best card, as it was always trump in "ombre," which succeeded "primero." Three players could participate in ombre, each receiving nine cards apiece. Trumps were named by the first player. James I liked "maw," which later became known as "five cards." In this game the five of trumps was the best card, the ace of hearts next, then the ace of trumps, and the knave. The ace of diamonds was the worst card unless diamonds were trumps. Two people could play this game—each receiving five cards. "Ruff" and "honor" required four players. Twelve cards apiece were dealt out, leaving four cards in the stack. The top card was turned up and its suit was named as trumps. The player with the ace of trumps could get the stack pile and discard four other cards. As in poker, the player bet on his hand in "post and pair." A poker face and a good bluff often won the game regardless of the cards held.

Dicing was popular and was more condemned even than cardplaying. Thomas Elyot's *Book Named the Governor* has little good to say of this form of play. "And I suppose there is not a more plain figure of idleness than playing at dice. For besides that therein is no manner of exercise of the body or mind, they which do play thereat must seem to have no portion of wit or cunning, if they will be called fair players." John

Illus. 19. Games requiring the use of dice. From Johann Amos Comenius, *Orbis sensualium pictus* (1685).

Illus. 20. Shovelboard. From *Le centre de l'amour* [1650?].

Northbrooke's treatise against dicing objects to it for similar reasons. To him only play which exercises the mind or body is permissible. He cites various laws against dicing but says that royalty sets a bad example, and certainly Henry VIII was an enthusiastic gambler. Nicholas Faret, giving instruction to young gentlemen in *The Honest Man,* indicated that they should know games at hazard, but they should not be gamblers, for as he says, "There are none but great princes (whose condition can never be miserable) which may abandon themselves boldly unto it [gambling]."

The most popular dice game was called hazard. In this game the thrower calls a number between five and nine before throwing. If he throws the number called or a number with a fixed correspondence to it, he "throws a nick" and wins. If he throws two aces or a deuce and ace he "throws out" and loses. If neither, he throws until the first number thrown (the chance) comes up and he wins, or the number first called (the main) comes up, in which case he loses.

Gambling took another form in betting, particularly on horse races. Public races were established by James I, and one of the famous races was the "Bell Course" race which had for a prize a silver bell.

There were other indoor games less harmful to the moral well-being of the participant. Among these was backgammon, called "tables" in Tudor times, probably because the board consisted of two tables hinged together. The ancient game of chess has been a favorite with contemplative men throughout the ages, though James I felt that, far from relaxing a person, chess filled his head with troubles. In England chess assumed its modern shape by Elizabeth's time, a little later than in Europe. Similar to chess was the philosopher's game in which the board was in the form of a parallelogram with squares marked. Instead of chessmen, the counters used had numbers on them. Each player had twenty-four counters, of which one was a king. The object was to take the opponent's king and make a triumph.

Shovelboard was played on a long table. The flat weights were shoved down the table to reach certain points. This is

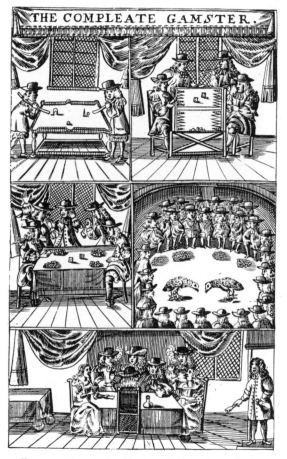

Illus. 21. Frontispiece from Charles Cotton's *The Complete Gamester* (1680), showing billiards, tables, dicing, cockfighting, and cards.

essentially the same as the shovelboard (or shuffleboard) played on board ship except for the use of the table.

Billiards in its modern form is not too different from the game known to the Elizabethans. The table was covered with a fine green cloth and had six pockets. One difference was that sixteenth-century players used a small ivory arch called a port which stood where the pyramid spot stands now; they also used an ivory peg called a king at the other end of the table. The players had two balls with which they tried to pass the port first and then gently to touch the king.

In the evening, for those men who preferred to pit their skill against the flashing eyes and nimble feet of a pretty girl, the music would sound and the dance would begin—either a "basse" dance in which the dancer's feet did not leave the ground or the "haute" dance which required hops, leaps, kicks, or stamps. A dance could be a dignified movement or a lively form of exercise. The pavan and allemande were stately dances, whereas the galliard and volta or lavolta were more lively. In many of the dances, as in the basse dance and the pavan, the man and woman danced side by side. The courante (sometimes spelled "coranto") presented another form, in which three couples in a straight line faced the onlookers, then each other, and finally turned around again to face the audience.

Dancing, however, was not approved by all. John Northbrooke described dancing as one of the evils of the world. In his diatribe he called this amusement "the vilest vice of all" and then went on to say that "truly it cannot easily be said what mischiefs the sight and hearing do receive hereby . . . ; they dance with disordinant gestures, and with monstrous thumping of the feet, to pleasant sounds, to wanton songs, to dishonest verses."

All sports did not require active participation. One of the favorite pastimes for all was a bearbaiting match or a cockfight. Cockfighting was an old sport. In the early days boys took a cock to their schoolmasters on Shrove Tuesday. Before the masters could claim the cocks, the boys were allowed to fight them in the yard. Or else they engaged in another pastime called

THE
Commendation
of Cockes, and Cock-
fighting.

Wherein is fhewed, that Cocke-
fighting was before the com-
ming of Chrift.

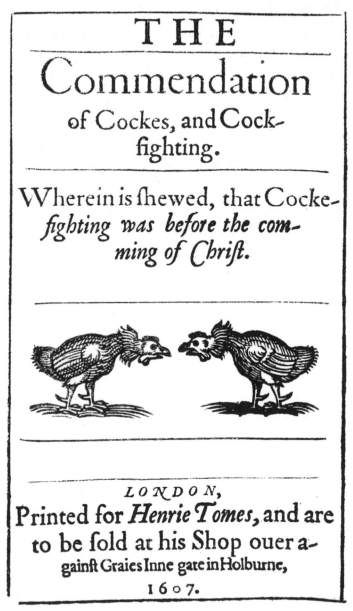

LONDON,
Printed for *Henrie Tomes,* and are
to be fold at his Shop ouer a-
gainft Graies Inne gate in Holburne,
1607.

Illus. 22. Title page to George Wilson's *The Commendation of Cocks* (1607).

cockthrowing, which involved throwing sticks and stones at the cock until it was killed.

The first cockpit was not built until the time of Henry VIII. He liked the sport so much that he added a cockpit to his palace at Whitehall. Drury Lane (or the old Phoenix) Theatre began as a cockpit. Philip Stubbes tells us that houses were erected for the purpose of cockfighting, that flags and pennants would fly on the day of a fight, and that proclamations were sent to announce the coming event.

Bearbaitings were often announced by a parade with the bearward leading the bears through the street, probably accompanied by music and jesters. As early as 1526 Paris Garden in Southwark became a popular resort for bearbaiting and bullbaiting. There the bear or bull was chained to a stake and four or six mastiff dogs were turned loose. As one dog was killed another was set upon the bear. The sight of tearing flesh and spilling blood accompanied by the yelps of the dogs and the growls of the bear evidently gave the crowds great pleasure, for the events were largely attended. Robert Crowley in *One and Thirty Epigrams* gives us a good picture of the event.

What folly is this, to keep with danger,
A great mastiff dog and a foul ugly bear?
And to this only end, to see them two fight,
With terrible tearing, a full ugly sight.
And yet me think those men be most fools of all
Whose store of money is but very small,
And yet every Sunday they will surely spend
One penny or two the bearward's living to mend.
At Paris Garden each Sunday a man shall not fail
To find two or three hundreds for the bearward's vail.
One halfpenny a piece they use for to give.
When some have no more in their purse, I believe.

These brutal sports were favored by royalty, aristocrats, and the lower classes alike. Cockfighting was highly favored by James I, and Elizabeth entertained the French and Danish ambassadors on two different occasions by attending a bearbaiting. The Puritans and the city aldermen objected to this sport, not for humane reasons but because of the disorderliness of the crowds who attended. Bearbaitings were usually held on Sunday, a fact that increased the disfavor of the Puritans. The city aldermen were opposed to any large gathering, for the plague was a bitter enemy and spread easily in crowded areas. It was not until many years later, when the conditions of life improved for many people, that these sports came to be looked upon as brutal. But in the sixteenth and seventeenth centuries, when it was a common experience to see hangings, beheadings, and victims burned at the stake, the sight of dogs and bears tearing at one another must have been only a mild form of amusement.

SUGGESTED READING

General works covering various sports and recreations include Joseph Strutt. *The Sports and Pastimes of the People of England*, edited and enlarged by J. Charles Cox (London, 1903), which, although written in 1801, gives a comprehensive picture of most pastimes from medieval times; other general works are Christina Hole, *English Sports and Pastimes* (London, 1949) and Dodgson H. Madden, *The Diary of Master William Silence: A Study of Shakespeare and of Elizabethan Sport* (London, 1897; 1907). Volume II of *Shakespeare's England* (2 vols., Oxford, 1916) has several chapters on the subject, with special attention to Shakespeare's knowledge. Each chapter has a useful bibliography. A seventeenth-century work on games of chance and some sports is Charles Cotton, *The Complete Gamester: or, Instructions How to Play at Billiards, Trucks, Bowls, and Chess . . . To which is Added the Arts and Mysteries of Riding, Racing, Archery, and Cockfighting* (London, 1674; reprinted with the title *Games and Gamesters . . .* (London, 1930).

Thomas Frost, *The Old Showmen and the Old London Fairs* (London, 1874) has several chapters covering the Tudor and Stuart periods, and James H. Bloom, *Folk-Lore, Old Customs and Superstitions in Shakespeare's Land* (London, 1930) supplies information about fairs and festivals as well as children's games.

Edmund H. Burke, *The History of Archery* (London, 1958) has a good chapter on "The Yeomen Bowmen." Roger Ascham's *Toxophilus* (1545) was reprinted in an edition by Edward Arber in his series of English Reprints (London, 1869). For more titles see Clement C. Parker, *Compendium of Works on Archery* (Philadelphia, 1950).

General works on fencing include J. D. Aylward, *The English Master of Arms* (London, 1956) and Egerton Castle, *Schools and*

Masters of Fence (London, 1893), which surveys various works on the subject and contains illustrations from sixteenth- and seventeenth-century works. George Silver's defense of the English method, *Paradoxes of Defense* (1599), was reprinted with an introduction by J. Dover Wilson (Oxford, 1933).

Several contemporary works on hunting and hawking have been reprinted: George Turberville, *The Noble Art of Venery or Hunting* with the title *Turbervile's Booke of Hunting, 1576* (Oxford, 1908); Thomas Cokayne, *A Short Treatise of Hunting* (1591; London, 1932); Edmund Bert, *An Approved Treatise of Hawks and Hawking* (1619; London, 1891); and a section from Richard Blome, *The Gentleman's Recreation* (1686) under the title *Hawking or Faulconry by Richard Blome* (London, 1939).

Gerald E. Bentley has recently edited the anonymous *Art of Angling, 1577* (Princeton, 1958), which has particular interest because Mr. Bentley believes it to be the source for much of Izaak Walton's more famous *Compleat Angler*. Gervase Markham, *The Pleasures of Princes, or Good Men's Recreations* (1614) and Colonel Robert Venables, *The Experienced Angler* (1662) have been reprinted in one volume (London, 1927).

Information on dancing will be found in Mabel Dolmetsch, *Dances of England and France from 1450 to 1600* (London, 1949), which gives a good account of the dances and how to dance them, with music. Several contemporary works have been reprinted: Jehan Tabourot [Thoinot Arbeau, pseud.] *Orchesography* (1588), edited by Cyril Beaumont in an English translation (London, 1925); Sir John Davies, *Orchestra* (1596), edited by E. M. W. Tillyard (London, 1945); and Henry Peacham, *The Complete Gentleman* (1622; Oxford, 1906), which covers other accomplishments as well.

Julian Marshall, *The Annals of Tennis* (London, 1878) is a complete history of the game and gives a description of courts and the rules of play. Kenneth Matthews, *British Chess* (London, 1948) has a chapter on "The Early Game in Britain." For information on cards see Cotton's *Complete Gamester*, already cited, William G. Benham, *Playing Cards* (London, 1931), and Edward S. Taylor, *The History of Playing Cards* (London, 1865). A good contemporary description of bearbaiting is given in Robert Laneham's account of the entertainment of Queen Elizabeth at Kenilworth in 1575, reprinted by F. J. Furnivall under the title *Robert Laneham's Letter* . . . (New York, 1907).